Haiku Humpday

#HaikuHumpday

Joanna R Gray

Reasonable Awesome

_____

_____

_____

© 2020 Joanna R Gray

All rights reserved.
No part of this book may be reproduced or used in any manner without the written permission of the copyright owner except for the use of quotations in a book review.

Cover design by Jenn Craycraft. https://www.behance.net/jenncray

Cover art by Catalina Bellizzi-Itiola.

The cover art is by Catalina Bellizzi-Itiola (CATAPHANT), a multi-disciplinary artist from Chicago, currently based in San Diego.

Cataphant focuses on oil paintings that point us to truths about the human brain & spiritual experience. She has built up a large body of semi-educational, semi-therapeutic paintings to help us all understand and share an experience of the world around us. She will be turning these into a book in the future. We chose her painting for the cover of #haikuhumpday because her art helps us learn to look at the world in new and exciting ways.

Follow her on Instagram or Twitter @cataphant or find her on Patreon to support her work.

Visit
www.ReasonableAwesome.com/haiku
for seasonal fun, nerdy games, and
occasional contests.

Find us on Instagram and Twitter
@ReasonableAwe

Thanks for playing #HaikuHumpday together.

Jon # Erin # @thehinkydonut Claire Southwell # @gleithart Garnett Leithart # @lisabeyeler Lisa Beyeler-Yvarra # @cataphant Catalina Bellizzi-Itiola # @jasmineIsrael Aki Olson # Katie Gouge # @truzzi Brittany Petruzzi # @b.esmond # Sharon O'Donnell # Marina Dow # @watersbelle Elizabeth Waters # @the_medoracle # Ruth Hoffmann # @Fraser_martens Fraser Martens # Joe # @anmidaludi # @houltonamy # @23camels Amaanda Keyes # Jenn Craycraft # @svnrck Savanah Rock # @samanthaannjones # Christian Ledezma # Naphtali Garfield # Charity # @roanoke834 Austin Hopper # Debbie # @alliemichelle # Drake # Debra White # Laura Storm # Christi Hester # @Jennifer_foxley Jennifer Foxley # Emily Nye Hoos # Katie Carbajal # @natskath Natalie Williams # Sophia # @Itshaewona # @therealrickcarter Rick Carter # @jilliankmf Jillian Nightingale # Zach # David # Kathryn # Ramiro # @Dannerman Dan # @_lilly_larson_ # Emma # Lana # @sweetlandfarmva

Table of Contents

Introduction	1
Pets & Animals	7
Our Favorite Stories & Heroes	15
People, Friendships, & Dating	23
Coffee & Naps	29
Food	35
Holidays, Seasons, & the Weather	47
My Cat	57
Adulting, Work, & Parenting	61
Travel	79
Everything Else	89
Your Haiku	109

Introduction

#haikuhumpday is a simple idea. Open the book. Flip through the pages. Hopefully you'll enjoy the poems. Best of all, though, join the fun and write your own.

Of course, these haiku mostly follow the 5-7-5 syllable pattern we all learned in grade school. But haiku are so much more than that. The cliche of haiku being about cherry blossoms fluttering in spring breezes, is true, but it's so much bigger. Bigger; even though (or perhaps because) the poem has such a small container. Haiku are supposed to be about nature, fleeting thoughts, actual feelings, descriptions of how a moment affects you, or how it hits your senses. I have learned that, with Haiku Humpday, we accidentally stumbled into the shadows of a grand tradition with some of the ironic observations and mild snark that fill these pages.

For a very approachable deep dive, check out "On Haiku" by Hiroaki Sato.

Haiku should talk about the passing of time, the ephemerality (that's six syllables right there!) of beauty, and the way happiness or sadness, triumph or failure is fleeting so you better notice these feelings and thoughts while they happen. The idea seems to revolve around capturing and responding to that fleetingness. This is where our cliche ol' friend the cherry blossom comes back into play. It's small, seasonal, vibrant, literally falls to the ground, and if you've ever been in an orchard at the right time, you know it is truly breathtaking. A cherry orchard in blossom is a thing of wonder.

And I hope this small collection helps you take the time to wonder.

I hope you find even a bit of that sense of wonder and appreciation in these haiku. I hope you use this book to practice your own observation skills. Practice noticing. Practice pausing. Find your fleeting thoughts and pin them down to the paper.

Use the prompts the way I am forced to week after week. #haikuhumpday is a game, but even more than that, #haikuhumpday is a frame of mind.

How to Use This Book

#Haikuhumpday started on a bored Wednesday in an office somewhere -- officially on lunch break, of course. And it has grown into a small following of those of us who like to find the wonder and find the joy in even the most mundane of things.

For those of you who haven't (yet) played along online, here's a quick explainer:

Each week, I post a theme to social media [on Instagram as @joannaRgray] using a Question/Answer box. Then, for each topic/question that y'all send in, I write a haiku as an answer during the next 24 hours. Sometimes, the haiku relate back to the broader weekly theme, but more often it's a springboard sending our thoughts in a slightly different direction for three lines.

And then it all goes away.

As a group, we have written some haiku on a wide variety of topics over the years -- I'm looking at you "stethoscope" and "platypus." Some of the topics y'all submitted, I had no idea what they were. And some of them I had to stop myself from writing multiples and going on and on. There are, in fact, several about my cat and several more about coffee. (And, strangely, more than one about mermaids?)

But, I'll let you in on a secret.

The trick of #haikuhumpday is not to be "clever" or particularly funny or original. The trick is to come up with something--anything--interesting to say about whatever is in front of you. The world is full of a glorious and wonderful diversity of ideas, people, phobias, hobbies, movies, foods, books, teams, places, and every one of us has a different combination of favorite and least favorite. We all love different things, we all know about different things. But -- and here's the delightful part -- we can all find at least 17 syllables worth of valuable observation in about just about anything.

The point is the surprise. The wonder. The point is that it could be anything.

I hope #haikuhumpday is a writing prompt for us all. Use it to fire up your imagination on a coffee break, use it on a road trip, read it at parties (well, if you throw that kind of party), put a copy in the bathroom (but don't read it in a bathroom on your road trip -- get out of there as quick as you can!). Open #haikuhumpday to get creative when you need a break from chores, give it to your kids who are readers, or to encourage the ones who aren't. Use #haikuhumpday in classrooms or in boardrooms. The list goes on and on. Anywhere you can be, you can find something to pause and notice; you can write haiku.

#Haikuhumpday is a simple idea. Open the book. Flip through the pages, read the poems. Best of all, though, join the fun and write your own. Use the lines provided and write a quick haiku about your favorite topic on each page.

Go on, Give it a try.

_____

_____

_____

Please share any haiku you write on social media so we can all join the fun.

Make everyday #haikuhumpday!

Visit
www.ReasonableAwesome.com/haiku
for seasonal fun, nerdy games, and occasional contests.

Find us on Instagram and Twitter
@ReasonableAwe

Pets & Animals

_____

_____

_____

Elephants
Blind men touch a wall,
a rope, and a tree. Learn to
value point of view.

Torrential Rain
Another plague that
I would rather have than these
damned ants in my house.

Hedgehogs
When it's time to play
make believe with garden pets,
avoid opossum.

_____

_____

_____

A Boxer Dog Named Calvin ;)
The best dog is more
than a good reason to take
a long walk daily.

Capybaras
Enigmatic yet
happy and cute. Sounds like the
perfect dinner date.

Dog Wearing Cone of Shame
Sad doggo is sad
and also knows he's playing
with your emotions.

Locusts
This morning I found
ants in my underwear drawer.
I prefer the plague.

Whales
Waving as they go
and wondering where they are
off to day-by-day.

Rescue Dogs
When you find a friend,
it's like coming home at last
and knowing it well.

Updog
Knock, knock, who is there?
I'll tell you because secret
secrets are no fun.

Sparrow
I love the way you
love the smallest creatures in
the world around us.

Dogs Playing in Snow
It's so easy to
make a dog happy. Let's all
channel that feeling.

Fledglings
Many people this
spring are watching tiny birds
grow up to be strong.

Shots
Like a bat out of
a brightly-lit cave, banish
fear and take a chance.

_____

_____

_____

Yaks
Look things up, see as much as you can. Most of all, please try to travel.

Black Raven
Strong coffee (or fizz drink) powers our days looking for shiny objects.

Ticks
If you think about the world too much, everything is gross and scary.

What Does the Fox Say?
Learn to understand those who sound different from us and the world's better.

Puppy Poop
Just because it's on your mind, doesn't mean it has to be on ours, too.

Okapi
Whenever you can, be the fantastic version of what you are. Yes!

Cheetahs Can Run Faster Than Your Car
Even if only for a short while, do all the greatness you can.

_____

_____

_____

Fishing Cats
It makes sense that cats
catch fish, even if it would
not occur to me.

Basset Hounds
The French have shared so
much with us over the years,
and do we thank them?

Red Panda
There are many ways
to be a bear, but the best
is to be yourself.

Hamsters
Domesticated
pets are great, but more work than
plants. But more reward.

Dog "Spins" For Treats
Round in a circle,
our pets wrap us up on their
little pinky toe.

San Diego Zoo
We hold places dear
for many reasons, mostly
the people we love.

Snail
Gliding up the stem
of the next rosebush is all
I want from this life.

_____

_____

_____

Platypus
Being this hard to
read is not great when it comes
to online dating.

Meerkat
I'll stay on lookout
so you can dance and sing with
all of our new friends!

Warthog
I bet I remind
you of that guy you saw in
that thing one time.

_____

_____

_____

Pufferfish
I don't want to get
caught. But if I do, hope to
land on fancy plates.

A Fly
Ha! I rub my hand
on your food! That's not all -- dare
you to look it up.

Hippo
I am more deadly
than the famous shark, but less
than the mosquito.

Hummingbird
They say I move fast
and that must be true, but it's
like y'all are so slow!

Hedgehog
I hope you can join
me in the countryside one
day! We will drink tea!

Flamingo
I will happily
decorate your drinks and stand
plastic in your yard.

Hedgehog
Yes, I am prickly,
but my cuteness more than makes
up for it, right? Right??

Armadillo
The first time you see
me in the wild, I bet you
think I am made up.

Blob Fish
"World's ugliest fish"?!
This has to be because you've
not seen me at home!

Skunk
Can we all share the
Great Outdoors? You don't scare
me,
and I won't spray you?

Honey Badger
Don't care. Don't care. Don't
care. Don't care. Don't care. Don't care.
Don't care. I don't care.

_____

_____

_____

Let me remind you
of the value of rambling
in woods when you can.

_____

_____

_____

Our Favorite Stories & Heroes

_____
_____
_____

The Sound of Music
Alpine hopes and dreams
told in song with a bit of
dance and puppetry.

Drama
Be careful out there,
kids, as you tell your story;
build up with kindness.

DisneyLand Newbie
The magic never
dies. No amount of rain can
spoil your parade.

_____

_____

_____

Sparkle Emoji
A handsome toothy
grin, polished plates, shiny car;
it's cartoon-fancy.

The Horse and His Boy
The story tells of
triumph over odds and fear
as you learn to trust

Persuasion
Things to be believed
may come and go, but people
are worth working for.

Iocane Powder
Does immunity
last if you don't recall? Time
to look for loose change.

Musicals
Jazz hands, memorize
the lyrics, and dance to tell
the poignant stories.

Shrek
Movies with lessons
can be really bad. But this one
stands the test of time.

Sandra Boynton
Finding new things to
love is a joy in every
age and phase of life.

Swamp Troll
The riddle-keeper
uses wiles to challenge
our chosen pathways.

Star Wars Land at Disney!
On the edge of a
galaxy far, far away
we look for heroes.

Space Mountain
Up, down, and through the
flashing lights, the ride (like life)
will come full circle.

Windy Wednesday
Be careful what you
tilt at; if you choose wrong, the
details fall apart.

_____

_____

_____

The Stone Table (A Deeper Magic)
Deeper than veneer
and stronger than iron beams,
magic made the world.

Expelliarmus!
Before you can break
the rules, it's important to
understand them all.

Pixar
Simple stories can
contain infinities with
talking fish and cars.

O.W.L.s
Every culture has
important rites of passage
to mark adulthood.

Azkaban or Alcatraz
Literary sites
in real life are some of the
best place for tourists.

It's LeviOsa. Not LevioSA
Having the right words
and saying them the right way
matters quite a bit.

Could Have Been Neville
Millions of tiny
choices, each building on the
past, build the future.

_____

_____

_____

Buzz Lightyear and Woody
Falling... with style
is easier when you have
good friends on your side.

Raiders of The Lost Ark
When life offers you
an adventure, you better
wear a fedora.

Mulan
Going after big
goals with purpose and vigor
is inspiring!

About Time
Live each day so that
you wouldn't regret being
caught in a time loop.

While You Were Sleeping
A blow to the head
can help you define your goals;
but don't try at home.

Robin Hood
This movie is the
closest Disney will ever
show true love and peace.

Court Jester
"The vessel with the
pestle is safe." There. I saved
you a lot of time.

_____

_____

_____

Baby Yoda
Welcome to our hearts,
may you never waddle off
or get too far lost.

LOTR Marathon
when the only way
is through, it's nice to have a
marching companion

Byzantine Emperor Justinian
The sixth century
counted dates different so now
we have two Easters.

Movies
When it's dark outside,
we have to light up our world
all the ways we can.

Showtunes
When your story needs
a bit of magic, tap your
hat and wave jazz hands.

Martin Luther
Ninety-five theses:
civil disobedience
with long term effect.

Teddy Bears
Tucked in for the night,
calm, cozy, and comforting;
not a scary mask.

_____

_____

_____

Security Blankets
Linus wants us to
outgrow our weaknesses and
coax out our greatness.

Curious George
Ideas given
to children can be the best
kind of ideas.

Amy & Beth March
Sometimes we learn the
most from how people treat
those in the background.

Sweyn Forkbeard
Hopefully, he's just
hungry for Viking food, not
feeling blood thirsty.

Clark Kent's Glasses
We hid behind the
everyday things to mask our
fear of achievement.

Going Commando
Bold choices are more
fun if you can annoy your
friends at the same time.

Ninja Turtles
Wouldn't we all be
better people if the prize
had pepperonis?

_____

_____

_____

Samwise Gamgee
In a world of war
and rumors of war, be the
one who carries on.

Aravis Tarkeena
Bravery and quick
wits will get you far away
from nasty old men.

Clair Huxtable
Back when shoulder pads
were cool, we all learned to stand
a little taller.

Leslie Knope
Unstoppable force
of good, creative, power
suits, teachable, loves.

Levar Burton
A voice of reason
in the overwhelming list
of library choice.

_____

_____

_____

People, Friendships, & Dating

_____

_____

_____

Board Games
Friends who compete share
a strong bond. Roll dice, draw card,
face life together.

Skepticism
If you think he's more
interesting than any
man you've ever met...

Ex-Boyfriends
Like a pile of shoes,
kick off men you are done with
and change for comfort.

Basketball Season
The things we all love
can be wildly different while
we cheer each other on.

People Who Wear Socks with Sandals
Uncles, dads, and more
people who have no shame all
inspire greatness.

Cold Feet
Running toward change and
yet afraid to take the leap,
we all can relate.

Change
In the midst of life,
those we love will anchor us
in all that we try.

_____

_____

_____

New Shoes
If you know what you're
looking for -- in shoes and in
life -- the hunt's a breeze.

Hope
Fruits of the spirit
are love, joy, peace, patience and
swiping past losers.

Curiosity
The Mars Rover is
looking for signs of smarts,
not a cute smartass.

First Dates
Hopefully, all the
quirks are the restaurant
and not the person.

Online Dating
Don't judge a box by
the label, but yes, judge by
the front seat selfie.

Dating
It's all about who
you meet and who you get to
walk away from, right?

Shooting Your Shot
When the time is right,
just give her weird compliments.
What could it hurt, right?

Blue Eyes
Wink, wink, nudge, admit
that certain eyes can make the
knees go weak sometimes.

Superhero Dads
Stereotypes are
the kind of thing to mow down
Like long grass in spring.

Mom
Selfless giver and
the place of peace after a
day of hard choices.

Astronauts
Go looking for more
beyond the last known places,
like deep sea divers.

John the Baptist
A voice alone can
echo in a new era
if you're brave enough.

Mom and Dad
They love us and feed
us, clothe and clean us, and
sometimes we say "thanks!"

Too Many Weddings
Let me join you in
celebrating how tired
we are of parties.

_____

_____

_____

My Great-Great-Grandma
Hundred years ago,
so much less was possible,
but she did it all.

Butterbeer
Here's to the ones we
celebrate with because shared
joy is the strongest!

_____

_____

_____

Coffee & Naps

_____
_____
_____

Coffee Tables
Hey, you have a truck!
Will you help me move this one
thing/chair/tent/sink/time?

Coffee Shop (but Not for Coffee)
Hip murals share warmth
to build you up and push you
out into the world.

Weariness
Well-deserved rest is
the best kind of rest of all
the wide world's options.

Stickers
So the cool kids can
recognize each other from
across hip cafes.

Coffee
Sometimes you need to
find the energy to sit
and even relax.

Sleeping 'til Noon
Get the rest you need
to tackle the task at hand
with grace and vigor.

Seattle
MOHAI, space needle,
Pike's place, ferries, rocky beach,
coffee, art, ice cream.

_____

_____

_____

Sunshine
About to go out
with a fresh cup of coffee
is the hope of spring.

Naps
I wish I could sleep
in small amounts. I try, but
wake up tomorrow.

Caffeine
It may seem to you
that I have a problem, but
I see solutions.

Iced Americano
Slurp and clink and stir
the straw as the cool caffeine
refreshes and chills.

Sleep... or Lack of It
Interrupted rest
is better than no rest at
all. I sure hope so!

Coffee Shop
Local, organic,
and missing the walls, but at
least they have parking.

Coffee
Tangy and somehow
smooth as it goes down, it's just
beans, heat, time, and wet.

_____

_____

_____

Coffee
When it's time for the
routines to change, try to take
some comfort with you.

Coffee
We traverse afar
to bring magic beans into
our homes and bloodstreams.

Baby Nap
Peace, calm and restful,
brings order to the daily
bread and circuses.

Iced Coffee on A Hot Day
The adult juice box,
making sad people happy
when the caffeine hits.

Sleep
Z Z Z Z Z
Z Z Z Z Z Z Z
Z Z Z Z Z

Sleep or Not Enough Sleep
Sunrise or sunset?
Seeing both on the same day
means adventure time!

Sleep
A body at rest
will remain as rest until
the baby cries. Truth.

_____

_____

_____

Food

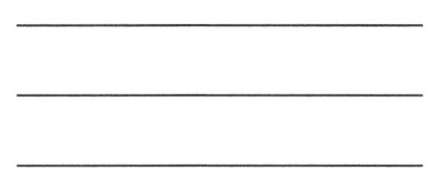

Chicken Nuggets
Of course, we eat the
legs first. Then the heads. Bodies
go last. Dino bites!

Julia Child
You've got to use the
courage of your convictions
to share what you love.

Chocolate Cake
Birthday every year
adds a candle, and makes it
less and less ice cream.

Coconut Milk
Gilligan's Island
gadgets keep the crew happy
'til the next plot twist.

Pickled Onions
Ok, sure, maybe
making onions stronger is
the missing flavor.

Grief
Like raisins when you
want wine & cheese, some parts of
life are a letdown.

Beets
Just because you're not
everyone's favorite doesn't
mean you can't be great.

_____

_____

_____

Menu Planning
Getting organized,
healthy, or rich; you get more
of what you plan for.

Pumpkin Spice
Sometimes, the way the
whole wide world loves this latte
makes me feel alone.

Smarties Candy
Pastel powdered sweet
untwist and krinkle, careful
not to drop the roll.

Pizza Rewarmed in A Microwave
Sad lunch happens. It's
extra sad when it's pizza.
Carbs in excelsis!

Pineapple
Hospitality
as it finest is when your
friends feel home in yours.

Pumpkin
Call me "punkin" one
more time! C'mon, I dare you!
You won't do it twice.

Parsnips
To perfectly roast
a vegetable is one of
life's great simple joys.

_____

_____

_____

Homemade Chicken Noodle Soup
Roasted, bones picked, hot
and ready to heal you from
what ails you today.

Molasses
You know the secret
to the best cookies revolves
around "made with love."

Sugar Wasted
Eating "just one more"
bite is how I ended up
feeling full of death.

Japanese Food
There's so much more than
sushi that I still have to
find the time to try!

Martinis
Fancy clink and sip
slowly to stretch the moment
and enjoy your toast.

Pizza
Pizza, pizza, the
magical food for all times
including today!

Hominy
Seeds of ideas
need to be roasted, to be
brought into new life.

_____

_____

_____

William Carlos Williams
This is just to say
that many fruits taste great when
they have been stolen.

Panini Sandwich
"Sandwiches near me"
is one of the more useful
phrases to search for.

Chicken Tenders!
Which came first? The egg
or the great lizard? Either
makes a good main course.

_____

_____

_____

Doritos
Classy snackers know
the best part of any chip
is the snappy crunch.

Ginger Root
Potent, long lasting,
and cheap. I wish more things were
like this humble plant.

Vegetables
The magic of
sun and dirt and time mixed up
to feed the whole world.

Celery Juice Craze
Anything can be
juiced or sold as a fad if
you squeeze it enough.

Plums
Sharp spikes scare off the
casual observer, but
life will grow sweetly.

Butter
Sunshine, sweet grass, time,
and the magic of a herd
of happy moo-ers.

Moldy Oranges
Sometimes you have to
take a risk and be open
to what lies within.

Sauerkraut
When boring cabbage
comes into each life, we must
learn to make it good.

Misophonia
Unwanted thanks from
happily munching friends, those
mannerless slackjaws.

Pineapple
When you know about
something this good, it's a shame
if you don't share it

Yogurt
A dash of sweetness
makes a healthy breakfast
smooth like creamy jazz.

_____

_____

_____

Burnt Hot Dogs
If you look away
for even a second, you
might ruin your lunch.

Eggs
As with most of life,
the things we take for granted
contain depths within.

Chicken Stir Fry
Comfort food while out
for healthy groceries is a
reason to smile.

Sour Cherry Pie
Sugar and tart, the
flaky crust is a sign of
mad skills at baking.

Angst
Put the lime in the
coconut and put off real
life til the morning.

Tiki Drinks
Try a fruity new
drink-y-drank and see what the
hub- is all a-bub.

Kitchen Nightmares
I won't tell if you
won't tell how long it sometimes
takes me to wash up.

_____

_____

_____

Waiting for Water to Boil
Respect the sea. You
know not what it may bring to
eat or be eaten.

Meal Prep
Sauté, sauté, fry,
dice, sear, chiffonade, blanch, bake,
or roast -- never boil

Hot Porridge for Breakfast
Looking forward to
a good breakfast is sometimes
reason to wake up.

Pumpkin Pie
Magic's in the crust.
No! The spices! No, it's the
everything of it.

Fudge Pie
Better than pudding
but so very many more
dishes to clean up.

Sweet Potato Pie
Many things that grow
and develop underground
become beautiful.

Moderately OK Chicken Parm
Among the many
joys of life, a little rain
must fall. Sorry, man.

_____

_____

_____

Grace Kelly and Cary Grant Eating Chicken in "To Catch a Thief"
Nothing builds up an
appetite like escape on
the Riviera.

Perfecting My Cinnamon Rolls
Knowing when to add
sugar, and when to add the
butter is wisdom.

Mushroom Soup
Start by sautéing,
add a bit of white wine, and find
delicious comfort.

Breakfast
Sliced avocado
scrambled eggs, diced veggies, and
never enough cheese.

Tofu
New food helps us find
flavor in our surroundings;
more of that this year!

Rum
And the happiest
of happy hours to you, too,
my gin-drinking pal!

Hot Drinks
Sometimes it's perfect,
the curl of a finger on
a mug of coffee.

_____

_____

_____

Pie a la Mode
In clothes or in crust,
following the fashion is
a matter of taste.

Raw Milk
We need to steward
what we've been given; happy
cows on happy grass.

_____

_____

_____

Holidays, Seasons, & the Weather

_____
_____
_____

Visit
www.ReasonableAwesome.com/haiku
for seasonal fun, nerdy games, and
occasional contests.

Find us on Instagram and Twitter
@ReasonableAwe

Sunny Rowboat
Strength and rest combine
in the proper working of
paddle-driven craft.

Rain
Grasping water is
a fool's errand. But we all
try it in our way.

King Cake
Of all the reasons
to go to church, Lent is a
secret favorite.

Advent Calendars
It is way too soon
to jump on this party bus,
but take me with you!

Weather
A reminder that
we're not in control of much
in our lives at all.

The Storming of The Bastille
The people will sing
as they breakdown walls, helping
all strangers seek peace?

Rain. So Much Rain.
The joy at the end
is part of the struggle now.
Don't ever give up.

_____

_____

_____

Raking
Skritt, scritt, crunch, scrunch, scrapt,
making a pile is a-
-nything but quiet.

Apples Taste Better After A Frost
Yet another way
I miss the fall somethin' fierce.
Please share it with me.

Parents' Candy Fee
We all have to pay
taxes. Let's have sugar-fun
while we all still can.

_____

_____

_____

Wedding Season
The best use of wide
open space is to fill it
with a big party.

Affection
Friends and family
gather to remember the
ways our lives are knit.

Dirty Feet
Spring days in winter
are a treat and a curse, as
we rotate wardrobes.

Spring
After dark and cold,
life comes bounding back in full
rejoicing colour.

Knitting
You tame chaos and
tie stylish knots to guard us
from the naked cold.

Rain
Too much of a good
a thing or at the wrong time is
not always so nice.

Rolling in Sunshine
Swings, mud pies, happy
children; are all the makings
of a happy life.

Magic
Brown, dead hillsides burst
into life as the rainy
season drys and ends.

Pollen
Breathing is urgent
when it gets more difficult.
Fresh air is priceless.

Overcast Days
We need to see the
darkness to know how good we
had it all along.

One of the Four Seasons
Vivaldi knows how
to convey temperature with
cat gut and horse hair.

_____

_____

_____

New Woodstove!
Gather round, take a
seat, share the warmth of the fire, good
friends and family.

Bocce Games and Rainy Days
If the weather don't
agree, ya gotta change the
way you plan your fun.

Cranberry Sauce
A good take on a
standard is always a good
and festive idea.

Some People Hate Candy Corn
My mouth is too full
of addictive corn syrup
to fight you right now.

Warmth
The summer sun comes
out stronger and stronger as
the days get longer.

Seasonal Allergies
I cannot wipe my
nose fast enough to keep up
with the air, today.

Sunburn
Being outside is
the best, and yet, it can kill
if you're not careful.

It's Too Darn HOT
When sitting still is
too much work, it's time to move
or take a beach trip.

First Autumn Rains
The weather breaks
and the world starts to reset;
readying for spring.

Fall in The Land of Perpetual Summer
Morning is cool, the
right kind of crisp, but midday
hits like hot blankets.

Snow in October
It's a surprise, but
not exactly the nice kind.
like fast shark attacks.

Salads for Summer / Soups for Fall / Baking for Winter
Seasonal food is
so nice from afar, for those
of us who have none.

Gorgeous, Crunchy Leaves
The best I can do
from my home by the beach is
to wear plaid PJ's.

Warm Surprise Sunshine
A break in the clouds
shines down to warm us before
the return of drear.

_____

_____

_____

Windshield Defrosters
To get the good times,
we much occasionally
scrape off the cold bads.

Snow Days
A semi-tropic
climate has benefits but
not festive weather.

Anniversaries
Row, row, row as time
and tide pass thru the days we
will remember best.

_____

_____

_____

Fish Sauce
Plan the flavors, line
up your prayers, look for the sun;
be Lenten aware.

Thanksgiving Break
The tasks before can't
outweigh the joy of the four
days of friends and food.

Traffic Jam
On this, the day we
all buy the same ten foods, it's
hard to stand in lines.

Awkward Parties
All parties improve
if you bring a dozen treats
to share... or liquor.

Packing Up Christmas
See you again next
year when it's time to put it
all back up on trees.

Feb 13th Is Awkward
When all the sugar
is filled with loneliness and
sad caloric-guilt.

Belated Birthdays
Extra days for us
to tell you how how great you
are! Wish I was there!

Sick Day
Don't let the sniffles
(or whatever worse ails you)
keep you down too long!

Ash Wednesday
One season each year,
pause, reflect. Mortality
is the path to life.

Happy Birthday!
I think you're neat from
your head to your feet and all
of you in-between.

Lent
Shaping the habit
of waiting and watching out
for new life to spring.

_____

_____

_____

Birthday
This flamingo hopes
your day is happy and that
you don't feel too old!

Dad's 60th Birthday
Flowers last a day;
men merely decades; but a
life well-lived will last.

18 Weeks 'til Christmas
Looking that far in
the future is a scary
kind of joyousness.

First Day of School Dread
Counting up or down,
the start of something new brings
all the ways to feel.

_____

_____

_____

My Cat

_____
_____
_____

Cats Usurping Humanity
As long as they don't
shut down all the restaurants,
I think we'll be fine.

Feral Feline Friend
This special blend of
trust and side-eye as I slip
through our shared spaces.

This Stray Cat
Trust is a value
only fully known when we
have fully earned it.

Cat
Sometimes, I like to
be totally calm, and then
sometimes, I do not.

Felix Felicis
With nine chances to
live life, make sure at least once
we try something BOLD.

My Apartment Full of Natural Sunlight
Like a cat curled up
in a slanted patch of warmth
we enjoy the sunshine.

Feral Cats
Caring for something
weaker than you is a sign
of nobility.

_____

_____

_____

Chasing the Cat
My morning routine
includes urgent meowing and
a little petting.

New Feline Friend
New cat haunts my lawn
and doesn't like to sit still,
so I talk gently.

Headaches
Lurking like a stray
cat, except we don't want this
phantom to settle.

_____

_____

_____

Adulting, Work, & Parenting

_____
_____
_____

Desk Plant
Orchid sets a goal.
Keep it alive and watch it
bloom. Plant or career?

Dirty Paint Brush
A sign of work well
done. Houses turned to home. It's
better when you share.

Spreadsheets
Organization
overload. Respect the one
who knows how to merge.

1st Birthdays
Day follows day and
we forget to notice 'til
suddenly it's now.

Old Injuries
Put your triumphs on
a pedestal and hold tight
to that strong feeling.

How Awkward It Is to Style a Scarf
It's just got to be
possible. I've seen other
ladies master it.

Fresh White Walls
Grown ups do this thing
where we care about the dust.
so we clean and paint.

_____

_____

_____

Screaming Child
Don't shake the baby,
even though he keeps awake.
Love the dimple-laughs.

Habits
Be careful how you
practice so you can get good
at being afraid.

Senioritis
Lord, help me reach the
end. And may I serve well my
brethren and sistren.

_____

_____

_____

Elections!
Clean up on all the
aisles! Bring your mops! Learn to
love one another!

Arthritis Flare-Up
Feeling stiff like a
statue and unable to
use fine motor skills.

Pilot Lights
Feeling pretty and
badassey when I think of
the furnace I lit.

Going Off to College
Hard work pays off with
more hard work if you're doing
it right. Adulting.

Sugar as Therapy
Three in the afternoon
is the best and worst time to
be in need of buzz.

Stethoscope
I cannot spell nor
do I know how to use. But
I am very grateful!

Blood on the Floor
And now I'm grateful
for the cleaning crews who work
behind the health scenes.

Forgetfulness
Making an un-made
the bed is the strongest habit
trigger that I know.

Pregnancy
Happy I get to
be a part of the cloud your
the family has here!

Job Hunting
Suffer the slings and
call backs of mortal toil.
Try to make a buck.

Go to The Dentist
A little prick of
fear amplifies the pain of
this unpleasant task.

_____

_____

_____

Managing Depression with Limited Resources
There are many "right"
answers in situations
like yours. Keep looking!

Cleaning the Bathtub.
It's ironic we
spend so much time cleaning a
small room full of soap.

Laundry
The one benefit
of the laundromat is that
it all gets done fast.

_____

_____

_____

Laundry
I wish all of life's
mysteries were simple as
"where's the other sock?"

How Is It Wednesday Already?
"No one ever lives
the same day twice." And "the days
are just packed." Fugit.

Kinks in My Back
These things happen as
we age no matter how we
keep active and stretch.

All the Toilet Paper in The Toilet
At least you have not
run out of this crucial thing…
well, I guess you have.

Babies
Bad maternity
leave policy is bad for
all -- not just new moms.

[no title]
Painkillers from the
bartender and the doctor
should never be mixed.

Done Being an Adult
Paying bills all-day
is less fun than I was led
to believe when young.

Public Restrooms with Toddlers
Just don't touch the walls.
Or the seat. Or the handle.
...anything really.

Clean My Bathroom
Hollywood has lied
about the glamour and the
glory of it all.

Teeth
Near the top of the
list of things I don't know how
to value enough.

Scans
Looking for signs of
life and ways to increase health.
Ask lots of questions.

_____

_____

_____

Weird Rashes
If you have spots, dots,
or squiggles, here's strong advice:
seek professionals.

Home!
Bloom where you're planted,
of course, but it's also good
to choose where you thrive.

Curls
Curled meats and cheeses
in styrofoam boxes make
the saddest desk-lunch.

_____

_____

_____

It's Too Early
I know. Some days are
days for big girl panties when
the alarm goes off.

Gross Sheetrock
We all have surfaces
we want to hide or improve,
as we grow and change.

Grading Papers
Red pen to say it's
good or could be gooder; to
shape young minds for life.

Internet Outages
So many things in
life have become the things we
all take for granted.

Orange Socks
May your socks support
you in your work as you stand
up against disease.

Cover Letters
Walking the fine line
between putting your best foot
forward and lying.

Little Boys Playing with Trains
When they are grown, look
to them for creative and
magnetic answers.

Snot. It's Everywhere
It's a dark day when
everyone is sick. Let's hope
we wake up healthy!

Library Story Time
This must be (by my
guess) one of the best parts of
being a parent.

Baby Playing with Old Oak Leaves
This is one of those
poetic ideas that
sound better than 'tis.

Playground Swings
That moment at the
top of the arc when you feel
both fear and freedom.

_____

_____

_____

Diapers
No matter how it
starts; food's the great leveler.
Everybody poops.

Awkward Coworkers
If you can't stop the
rain of comments, make up an
office drinking game.

Conference Call Failure
Look out! Your level
of distraction is on blast.
Who's the weakest link?

Typos
The higher the stakes,
the sadder it is when we
miss the target. Right?

Going to Bed Early
Finishing the day
with enough checked off to rest
is old lady joy.

Learning
Always be learning
so you'll never fall behind
is stressful success.

Mopping the Floor
Some things cannot be
avoided. Both death and the
tax man clean things up.

_____

_____

_____

Reorganizing Closets
If it brings you joy
and you have space, please make room
for all striped sweaters.

Toes
Well-supported toes
and heels keep the world going
around day by day.

Sad Lunch
I can't hate too much
about a free lunch from the
office snacks. No shame.

Night Shift
We expect too much
from too few when we set the
work expectations.

Dilemma
Time to improve or
buckle down? We must learn to
try another way.

Lonely Office
Having friends at work
makes make things better, let's
come in tomorrow.

Laundry Day
Everybody makes
a mess all around the world
and cleans up weekly.

_____

_____

_____

Server Mice
Computer code can
both build and destroy. The trick's
knowing which is which.

45+ Hour Work Week
This is your lucky
week, I guess. Otherwise it's
just a lot of work.

Working Nights
There are so many
people who work so hard to
make our lives better.

_____

_____

_____

Names
Behind every door,
a new friend waits. All that's left
is to knock, meet, share.

Painting
We are programmed to
make things better and you, my
friend, are an inspo!

Career Change
It's time to unplug
and try some new things to learn
what I want to do.

Endings
The time has come to
move to a better way to
spend my waking hours.

How Is It Not Friday Yet?
Take a nothing day,
turn it with a smile. Gonna
make it after all.

Student Loans
The small triumph of
a long string of on-time checks
is a very mood.

Make It Work
If there's something in
the way, success lies with those
who know how to bend.

Mowing the Grass
Straight line and turn back,
another straight line, and it
starts making us sneeze.

Management
When the shipment goes
wrong, but you're your own admin,
it's time to call mom.

Cyber Space Is Travel, Right?
Moving the facts and
figures over the web tubes,
we can see the world.

Getting Off Work Early
Get out your leisure
garments and get this weekend
off to a good start!

_____

_____

_____

What Are You wearing?
When your work shows on
Your clothes, it's living proof of
a hard job done well.

Schedule Conflicts
Torn between options
and unwilling to miss out,
or get enough sleep.

CPR Certification
Thank you for learning
these life-saving skills so we
can all breathe easy.

_____

_____

_____

Multiple Morning Alarms
You speak as if you
know the thoughts that live inside
my head all mornings.

Waiting on Hold
In an infinite
loop with no other options,
and so we all wait…

Migraine
Pinching, piercing, all
the way around each eyeball
with a hot ice pick.

Lazy Days Off
There are the days we
crave but often fear we might
waste it after all.

Old Notebooks
I rarely make it
more than a few pages in
before I start anew.

Start of The School Year
A fresh start is a
deep sign and jumping off the
cliff into the work.

Sehnsucht
When what you want can
be described in German, it's
getting serious.

I Don't Want to Work, but I Have a Mortgage
When you feel like you're
not making progress, at least
you're not on standby.

Not Enough Hours in a Day. So Busy!
Running so fast you're
inventing new ways to move
and still -- need to pause.

Work Life Balance
It's got to be the
worst when it's your job to make
someone else's fun.

Interview and New Hires
Firm handshakes, printed
resumes, discuss money,
and make good choices.

_____

_____

_____

Multilevel Marketing
Pants are lit, and the
Tupperware keeps it fresh, but
it's all just hot air.

Starting a New Career Path
Stepping out bravely
into the unknown armed with
skills, talent, and goals.

Car Registration Too Damn Expensive
One approach would be
to take the bus. You better
get some good headphones!

_____

_____

_____

Mop My Floors Regularly
Give the kids wet socks
and turn up the stereo.
Dance party til clean!

Save Up $30k
You mean you're not yet
a small business mogul with
podcast and book deal?

Spouse Got Two Job Promotions
After hustling
with (I assume) a smile,
we all say congrats!

Toilet Scrubbing
If you think about
it too much, indoor plumbing
is a weird concept.

Sweeping
Keeping our shiny
things shiny requires a
lots of investment.

Runaway Toddlers
Chasing through the days
of mud, and sticks, down toy truck
roads lined with play doh.

**The Disorientation of Coming
Back to Work After Two Days Off**
I recommend a
week by the beach. If not that,
lime plus coconut.

**Made It Through Some Real
Tough Times and Am Thriving!**
You did a good job,
you didn't give up, and that
is success. Always.

Payroll Taxes
Here lies blackness and
death to any who plumb the
mysterious depths.

Got Two Research Grants!
I can't wait to learn
the easy version of what
you get to study!

Build Your Own Future
Does it really cost
less if it costs you all of
your pieces of mind?

_____

_____

_____

Cleaning an Operating Room
You are doing what
is right and good as you care
about gross details.

But Did You Die?
Muddling through is a
totally acceptable
way to live your life.

_____

_____

_____

Travel

_____
_____
_____

Waiting for July Vacation
The work of saving
is rewarded when it comes
time to spend it all!

Rick Steves
Back in ye olde days,
we used to look things up in
books. Or call a friend.

Rear View Mirrors
Tricky parking lots
require vigilance and
lots of neck turning.

Seattle
When you don't mind the
rain or the traffic, it's time
to plan a visit!

Pop Up Tents
The REI sale
ends at midnight and gets you
to many trail ends.

Starbucks
The comfort comes in
because the options are the
same, no matter where.

Playgrounds
My favorite part
of any hotel is the
waffle maker thing.

_____

_____

_____

Post-Vacation Colds
Any excuse to
sit in pajamas all day
is a good excuse.

Twinkle
Pitch and roll, lookout
through the porthole, to the stars
that shine o'er us all.

Roadside Chicken
Trying new food and
finding a new favorite
is one of life's joys.

_____

_____

_____

I Want to Go to There!
Free jazz combo in
the sculpture garden of a
museum? Yes, please!

House Guests
When your friends have the
wifi already saved in
their phone, that's comfort.

Romania
The farther afield
we wonder, the more we see
more places to go.

Dirty Feet
Our feet take us all
over the world and give us
the great adventures.

Funny Anecdotes
"You just had to be there!" only gets you so far out of a plot hole.

Scammers
Border crossings would be one of the worse places to lose your ID.

New Beginnings
A week on the beach is the way we reset. Or so I have been told.

Road Trips
There are a million reasons to value freedom and time to travel.

When Friends Come to Visit
Long distance is a joy and a trial; so we collect airline miles.

Road Trip/Biking/Camping/ Stargazing/Sunsets/Family
Your list gives off a strong mix of jealousy and the desire to nap.

Windows & Light
Keep our eyes on the horizon to see what's next as we travel on.

_____

_____

_____

Having Little Money to Travel
To enjoy where we
live should be embraced as a
truly special skill.

The Haze of Distant Hills
Like a magnet for
the soul, mountain paths call us
to the heights and depths.

Flying Cross-Country
Keep your head up and
look out ahead for good views;
you'll be ju-uuust fine.

_____

_____

_____

Traffic Jams
The red and green lights
are festive and all, but think
they control so much.

Travel Plans
Train whistles, anchor
chains, and engines revving are
some of the best sounds.

Traveling Tomorrow!
Don't forget to send
me a postcard when you get
to where you're going.

The Mackinac Bridge
Road trip marker on
the way to fun or the way
back home afterwards.

Distance
Just put one foot in
front of the other and you
are unstoppable.

Public Transit
When walking just won't
do, we flag a bus or hop
a train. Get there slow.

Australia
I have never been
but I would gladly get on
a plane. Who's paying?

Long Distance Driving
You have found one of
my favorite ways to pass the
distance and the time.

The Yellow River
Today I learned that
the Yellow River is not
the Yangtze River.

Traveling
Many reasons to
wander as we seek out a
better life or week.

Road Trip + Toddlers
I hope your weather
is fitting for stretching at
rest stops and more snacks.

_____

_____

_____

Road Trips
Pick a good playlist
and settle in for a long
stretch between stretches.

Catchy Songs
Earworms take over
and fill your consciousness with
joyful melody.

Boarding Airplane
The urge to travel
is nearly as strong as
the urge to return.

Seattle
Up where it's green, where
it rains all year and coffee
is strong and local.

New Car Smell
The automotive
equivalent of axe spray
shouting out, "I'm fancy!"

Camping
To get out of doors and
stay a while cures the souls as
well as the body.

Broken AC in the Car in TX
Some situations
will get worse before they get
better, unless fixed.

_____

_____

_____

Settling Into A New City
Welcome! Hopefully
you will quickly learn to call
these new places "home."

On a Boat
May we all get the
chance to be the one who shows
up sharing good toys.

The Oregon Coast
In the place where the beach
meets forest, we can reset
for the work ahead.

Small Lake with Pine Trees
Crunching on needles,
sinking into sand, waves tease
the hem of your shorts.

Everything Else

_____

_____

_____

Salute
Me? Patriotic?
Yielding to a fire truck
feels better than flags.

Short Story
Hobby? Or escape?
Kite on a skyscraper roof
climbs the corp ladder.

Night
Streetlights make me feel
safer, but the light pools up
to highlight the dark.

Smoke
Pray for rain to quench
the fiery spirit into
manageable s'mores.

Reconnecting After Loss
Unpack old baggage
to learn how to rebuild a
life still worth living.

Podcast
The future's gonna
be a wild ride full of
tech and new hobbies.

Rain
Things that rise will float
slowly down; decor from a
past baby shower.

_____

_____

_____

Harvest Haze Makes Mountains Prettier
All windows can look
out. But what you see depends
on what you look for.

Changing Viewpoints
Don't take for granted
ideas you've got by proxy.
Don't believe the hype!

Beard Stubble
5 o'clock shadow
is difficult to maintain;
or so I am told.

Expired
It's time to get up,
learn humility, get woke,
and treat others well.

Neighborhood Jackhammers
Progress sometimes feels
like it moves backwards before
moving toward greatness.

Empty House
The quiet stillness
before the crowd descended and
makes the house a home.

Jogging
Follow each path where
it leads and you're likely to
have the most fun. Run!

Flowers with Dew on The Petals
So fresh and so clean
and a new perspective on
all of life's questions.

Wind
The more that we stretch,
the wind can blow and we bounce
back from breaking points.

Hair
Spikes, curls, or a weave;
hairs and how to care for them
stress me the heck out.

Sore Throat. Possibly Getting Sick
You can't let the germs
win! Keep hydrated and find
some warm chicken soup.

More Gray Hair Than I Can Count
Gray hair causes stress,
but living a life of lies
is more unhealthy.

Yoga Class
Centering on calm,
strength, and growth working on goals
both body and mind.

The Spanish Inquisition
Decisions based on
bad intel have a clear track
record of failure.

_____

_____

_____

Intrigue
To lead those into
uncharted territory
who want to know more.

Dance
In the rain or the
ballroom, pursue the things that
give you easy joy.

Orchids
Some things start out good
and then get complicated.
don't be a weird growth.

Social Awkwardness
When people get close
but you just can't leave, you have
to learn to love them.

Bathroom Shelves
How do you roll your
most important papers and
keep those things handy?

Fortress
Bricks and buttresses
will go down in history
if we don't ruin.

Walmart
Super or not, when
it's all you know, options look
better than they should.

_____

_____

_____

Benadryl
Too much of a good
thing sometimes makes us immune
to all the goodness.

Old Friends
To know and be known
is a great gift. Without it,
there's a you-shaped hole.

Too Many Squats
Be careful what you
try. People get addicted
to lots of weird stuff.

Palm Trees
I don't know what they
give to us except a sense
of joy and wonder.

Drugs (The Happy Kind)
I hope everyone
gets the help they need and that
their friends show them love.

Bronchitis
Motherhood must be
scary. You have to know so
much about so much.

Fashionable Lateness
Never bother with
people you'll hate. Dinner's at
eight. Don't be a tramp.

_____

_____

_____

80s Hit "Africa" by Toto
Ok, sooooo the more
times I listen to this song,
the less sense it makes. :)

Kaleidoscope
Twist around and slide
with childhood eyes to see the
world in all new ways.

Avoiding A Cold
Stay at home and click
on mouse or remote work. Don't
spend time out with friends.

Fluffy Blankets
To be at home and
the comfort of knowing you
are done for the day.

Dry Shampoo
The things we ladies
do for the sake of moments
more of sleeping in.

Broken Bones
Some things can be fixed
but never fully back to
how we started out.

Fear... of Losing
They say you miss one
hundred percent of all the
shots you do not take.

_____

_____

_____

Putting Down Roots
Floating in air or
water makes it tricky, but
worth every effort.

Analysis Paralysis
I hope the things that
give you pause range from good to
even more goodness.

Boredom
If you're looking for
a way to fill your spare time,
may we suggest chores?

Late
We're all mad here! And
the best cure is to give each
other lots of grace.

A Very Bad Cold
Incoherent thoughts
are all we have today, but
let's still do this thing!

Photography
Combining letters
into words and phrases is
communication.

Dry Shampoo
In this time of change
and life events, this may be
the most shattering.

_____

_____

_____

H2O
Wetness, steam, and ice
can all serve as ways to see
the world we live in.

Crayons
Stay creative, move
fast, and try not to break things
as we live our days.

Theater
We play pretend to
make the world less scary and
act like all is fine.

National Haiku Day
Taking the time to
notice details and give the
best ideas voice.

Sewing
The skills we can share
are part of how we can bring
joy to those nearby.

Biking
Roll past and smell spring
blooms mixing with the scent of
Mercedes exhaust.

Death by Head Cold
Compression, pressure,
sniffles and a headache make
this a slow, sad death.

_____

_____

_____

Sprouts
The beginnings are
so exciting; anything
at all can happen.

Barber Shop
How can the finished
cut look so bad when the shop
is the hippest place?

Nail Polish
The smallest things are
only small is you let them
remain unnoticed.

Beanbag
Gathered together,
we play and eat and toss the
ol' bags into holes.

Mermaid
If you met one, how
would you react? With joy or
fear? Or cameras?

Planters Warts
A wart by any
another name will still break the
fairy tale curses.

Puzzles
Over, around, and
under, and through -- never stop
looking for good paths.

_____

_____

_____

Movement
The more I see a
a thing done really well, the more
I won't move backwards.

Pool
Floating in silence
with a slight splash reminding
of the world outside.

Flooding
Slowly dripping through
each and every crevice
to wreak all havoc.

Mermaid
To thrive in more than
one world requires that we
have respect for both.

Pottery
Balance, stretching, heat.
a little bit of each will
make us all stronger.

Morning Dew
Like magic, the dry
ground produces water for
the daily struggle.

World Peace
If all you can do
today is make one person
smile, that will do.

_____

_____

_____

Paddle Boards
Splash and reach but take
care not to over-extend
to a new hobby.

Keys
Open doors and hearts
as we daily lay down our
lives for each other.

Polka Dots
Classic Swiss, multi-
color, shapes and patterns, or
with Minnie Mouse ears.

Messenger RNA
Making coded plans
to build the future: passing
microscopic notes.

Reparations
Mama always said
to fix the things you broke and
this might be the worst.

Chain Link Fence
They say, "good fences
make good neighbors," but I'd like
to see more cookouts.

Crooked Cactus
The right approach to
prickly bits of life can be
turned into support.

What Kind of Feminist Are You?
I hope you're the kind
who won't be ignored, like a
pebble in the shoe.

_____

_____

_____

Water Balloon Fights
Smile while running
through the lawn and over the
made up lines of war.

Shimmery Palm Trees
Rustling in a soft
breeze, making the gentle sound
of warming and sunshine.

Paint
Even if you're not
all that skilled, get out there and
express emotions.

Half Square Triangles
With a blend of math
and fabric, you make a plan
and keep your folk warm.

Plant Slumber Party
You bring me even
more shades of color and shapes
of leafy goodness!

Rock Climbing
Teaching yourself to
get up and get off the ground
is a top life skill.

Embroidery
Adornment is not
useless; it's the way we make
the world beautiful.

_____

_____

_____

Sweet Potato Plants in Pots
Gardening is not
glamorous, but it's one of
our best ideas.

Surfing
You paddle and pause,
waiting for the world to line
up in pleasant ways.

Cleaning
Vines climb up even
if the situation is
less than then ideal.

Guitar Practice
Hold tricky poses
past the point where your fingers
hurt and you are done.

Sprained Ankles
Here's to the strength it
will take as you daily crush
death beneath your heels.

ER
If I am broken,
please don't call an ambulance.
I'll buy a new car.

Cozy Fire
Every place we live
has a different way to show
warmth and radiance.

_____

_____

_____

Help
Now is the time for
all of us to come to the
aid of our neighbors.

Care
Comfy slippers, paired
with a cup of coffee and
a favorite doughnut.

Swim Lessons
In pursuit of bold
goals, one must do unpleasant
tasks, like gym showers.

_____

_____

_____

Head Cold
Without even the
the satisfaction of a good
cough to clear things out.

Estranged Family Relationships
Cling to the promise
we'll be made whole before the
the world comes to an end.

To Bail on a Commitment or Not?
Sometimes we have to
suck it up and do things we
hate. But not always.

The Pythagorean Theorem
I am the very
model of liberal arts grads:
have forgotten lots.

How It Feels with a New Book
Anticipation
grows, with dread hope, that the end
does not let us down.

Contemplative Prayer
Slow down and follow
someone else's lead through the
pathways of your mind.

Controlled Chaos
When it looks like it's
all about to go to bits,
is when it's "just right."

Besmirched
I don't know who needs
to hear this, but it's time to
clean your eyeglasses.

Poop
From dust, we are built
and to dust, we shall return,
with "ish" in between.

Roller Coaster
Over, around, through
thick, thin, good, bad and blessings:
LIFE COMES AT YOU FAST.

Breathe Well
It's the things we take
for granted that we need to
practice noticing.

_____

_____

_____

Jump
A dance, a graceful
escape, to scale a wall, or
clear every hurdle.

MadLibs
An attorney and
a priest walks into a bar
and the barkeep says...

Frigid
Uninsulated
walls are keeping me colder
then would be ideal.

_____

_____

_____

Ardent
A word that sounds old-
fashioned but really it's quite
young and passionate.

Filibuster!
When you've something worth
defending, use all the words
you know how to say.

Choir
Voices raised, open
mouths weaving in and out of
a rollicking fugue.

Peace and Blessings
I hope we all have
a place, a blanket, or mug
to bring simple peace.

Deadlines
A date, a star, a
the bright line in the sand calling
us to finish strong!

Dreams
If your recurring
dream is a floating laser
show… maybe wake up?

Your Shoes
Go out and explore,
lace-up and keep trying to
climb up higher heights.

New Boots
Click your heels, straighten
your spine and walk tall, even
while breaking them in.

_____

_____

_____

Your Haiku

_____

_____

_____

Please share any haiku you write on social media so we can all join the fun.

Make everyday #haikuhumpday!

Visit www.ReasonableAwesome.com/haiku for seasonal fun, nerdy games, and occasional contests.

Find us on Instagram and Twitter @ReasonableAwe

_____
_____
_____

_____
_____
_____

_____
_____
_____

_____
_____
_____

_____
_____
_____

_____

_____

_____

_____
_____
_____

_____
_____
_____

Reasonable Awesome

Visit
www.ReasonableAwesome.com/haiku
for seasonal fun, nerdy games, and
occasional contests.

Find us on Instagram and Twitter
@ReasonableAwe

_____

_____

_____

www.ingramcontent.com/pod-product-compliance
Lightning Source LLC
Chambersburg PA
CBHW081507080526
44589CB00017B/2683